GW01605310

A Purnell book
ISBN 0 361 03856 9
First published 1977. Reprinted 1987

Printed by Purnell Book Production Ltd
Paulton, Bristol. A member of BPCC plc
Macdonald & Co (Publishers) Ltd
Greater London House, Hampstead Road
London NW1 7QX. A BPCC plc company

RUPERT

and the Swift Journey

Illustrated by Paula Cox
Based on an original story by Frederick Chaplain

Purnell

CHAPTER 1

Rupert looked out of the window one morning to see the rain pouring down and splashing off the gutters on the roof. It really was a very wet day.

"Oh dear," he thought in dismay. "I probably won't be allowed to go out and play in this weather."

Half an hour later, just as Rupert had decided to play with his toys, a tiny patch of blue appeared between the storm clouds, and a watery sun shone down on the puddles.

"I think it's going to clear up, Mummy," cried the little bear. "Can I go out and play now?"

"Well, yes, dear," smiled Mrs Bear. "You'll

have to wear your wellingtons though, as it will be some time before the ground dries out."

Rupert hurried off to put on his shiny black wellington boots, and as soon as he was ready he ran outside into the sunshine and immediately jumped, with a great big splash, into the biggest puddle he could find.

"Oooh! This is fun," he shouted, sliding on a patch of mud.

"Now you just take care, Rupert," called Mrs Bear from an open window. "I don't want you coming home covered in mud."

Rupert waved merrily at his mother, and promising that he would be careful, he ran off splashing through every puddle he came

to, and sending silvery sparklets of water around him as he went.

He was so absorbed in his new water game that he almost bumped straight into his little chum, Pong-Ping, who was standing completely still in the middle of a rather large puddle.

"Hullo, Pong-Ping," exclaimed Rupert. "I

say, I'm sorry I very nearly knocked you over. Did I splash you?"

Pong-Ping didn't answer straight away, and Rupert noticed that he was holding a small radio very close to one ear and listening intently.

"Hullo!" screeched Rupert at the top of his

voice. At this sudden loud noise Pong-Ping jumped in fright.

"Oh, it's you, Rupert," he said with relief. "You quite startled me."

"Well, you must be very interested in the programme on that radio," replied the little bear. "You didn't even see me coming, and do you know that you're standing in a big puddle–your shoes look very wet to me."

"Oh dear!" gasped Pong-Ping. "I just didn't see it. I was too busy listening to the news. You'll never guess what I've heard! They've just announced on the news that some rare dragons have been spotted. They're little dwarf dragons. Here, listen!" He handed the radio across to Rupert, who listened carefully with a puzzled expression on his face.

"Oh," he said after a minute. "I'm afraid I've lost it. All I can hear is a faint buzzing and crackling."

"That's because the battery is so old," replied Pong-Ping. He giggled suddenly. "Rupert, did you know that *you're* standing in a puddle now?"

"That doesn't matter," laughed Rupert. "I can stand in as many puddles as I like, because I'm wearing wellingtons."

The two chums walked along side by side, while Pong-Ping related all the details he had heard about the dragons.

"They've just been discovered in a place called Nexdor," he said excitedly. "They are very strange creatures. You know that dragons usually breathe fire, don't you? Well," he smiled, "*these* dragons breathe electric

sparks! Come with me, I want to show you something."

Still puzzling over the idea that dragons could breathe electric sparks, Rupert followed his little pal to his mansion, where Pong-Ping immediately led the way to the garage. Unlocking the garage door, he said, "I simply must get one of those dragons for a pet. I shall go today."

Rupert was startled. "Do you mean straight away? You're going now?" he asked.

Pong-Ping grinned as he opened the garage door. "Well, almost straight away," he said briskly. "As soon as I've made a few preparations. I can get there and back in a day in my go-anywhere-car, you know."

Rupert gasped at the odd-looking machine which was now revealed to him.

"Goodness me, is that it?" he said. "It looks like a tractor."

"It's certainly not," snorted the little peke. "Look, it's not as heavy as it appears. It was made for me by a very clever inventor," he went on proudly. "It's made of a light metal, and it will go on land, sea and air!"

As Rupert wandered around the amazing machine, his friend explained how it worked.

"It is driven by powerful jets," Pong-Ping told him. "I've only had it a few weeks. Just wait until you see how fast it goes. We'll be in Nexdor in no time at all."

"We?" repeated Rupert, in surprise. "Do you mean that I'm going too? I didn't *say* I was going with you."

"Oh, but of couse you're coming," replied Pong-Ping airily. "I'm sure you've never been on a dragon hunt before. You'll really enjoy it. Besides," he went on, as he fiddled with the controls, "I need someone to help me. They're very tricky creatures to catch, these dragons."

CHAPTER 2

Rupert was a bit nervous at his friend's suggestion.

"B-but where is this place called Nexdor?" he faltered. "It sounds as if it's an awfully long way away."

"Certainly, it's a long way," replied Pong-Ping with a smile. "Look," and he spread out a map on a bench and waited while Rupert studied it.

"Why, it's a foreign country, and it's miles and miles away!" gasped the little bear in dismay. "I couldn't possibly go with you. Mummy would never let me go that far."

"It will only take us a day to get to Nexdor and back," replied Pong-Ping with a grin. "I won't accept any excuses."

"It's no good, Pong-Ping," said Rupert. "I shall have to ask Mummy, and I'm quitc sure she won't let me go with you, although it *would* be exciting."

"I know," said Pong-Ping. "Leave it to me, Rupert."

As the little bear looked up in surprise, the peke added with a smile, "You're coming to Nexdor. I have to see a friend about a special dragon collar before I go. On the way, I'll call and ask her if you may go with me. I am sure I can persuade her that it's all right. While I'm away, you could help me by polishing the car. There's a duster in that cupboard there, and an oilcan too, if you feel like oiling it as well."

"Fancy him thinking Mummy will let me go," Rupert thought. "Of course she won't. That place called Nexdor is much too far away."

Nearly an hour later, Pong-Ping returned, carrying a small collar and chain.

"It's all right, Rupert," he shouted breathlessly. 'It's all arranged. Your Mummy doesn't mind so long as you're back in time for tea."

Rupert was astonished by his friend's news. "Are you sure?" he gasped. "Did Mummy *really* agree?"

"Yes, yes, it's all fixed," replied the peke, briskly. "Now come on, we've got to get going. This collar will be just the thing," he added. It's specially made for dragons that breathe

electric sparks and flashes, but I'll tell you more about that later. Let's hurry and get ready!" He seemed to have forgotten all Rupert's fears in his eagerness to set out, and without giving his friend any time for second thoughts, he started passing things to Rupert to load into the machine. They took some food for the journey and Pong-Ping produced a large tin marked 'Dragon Food', which he stowed carefully in the back of the car.

"I'll just tie a piece of this to a long cord," he said with a chuckle. "It will coax one of the dragons just near enough for us to catch it. They can't resist this stuff, you know. And now I think we're ready to go," declared the little peke, and clambering aboard the go-anywhere-car, he settled himself in the driving seat.

"Climb in, Rupert; you'd better take the back seat. We'll be travelling very fast today, so you'll need to hold tight when I tell you. There's a strap on your seat, so that you can fasten yourself in."

CHAPTER 3

Rupert climbed into the machine behind his chum, and with a deep rumble the engine started. Guided by Pong-Ping, the car roared through the grounds of his mansion and then lurched out across the open fields, gathering speed all the time. The little bear was getting used to the whining sound of the wind whistling past his ears, and was suddenly surprised to notice that they were approaching a steep slope at great speed. Pong-Ping drove straight towards it and shouted back to Rupert, "Here we go! Get ready to hold on!"

The trees were going past in a blur and Rupert felt the car tip as it started up the slope at an amazing pace. Too scared to reply he clung on with all his might and shut his eyes tightly. At the very crest of the hill there was a violent explosion from the rear of the car, followed straight away by another and another. Rupert opened his eyes.

"Goodness, what was that, Pong-Ping? Are we blowing up?"

"Don't worry!" yelled the little peke. "It's just the jets. I've switched them on." And Rupert gasped for breath as the car shot straight off the top of the hill into the air.

"That's a jolly good runway," chuckled Pong-Ping, looking back at Rupert's scared expression. "It's all right. Look, you can see the whole of Nutwood spread out below us."

"My, you can see for miles and miles," Rupert gasped. "Why, it's wonderful, Pong-Ping. Now I know that your car can really fly, I think I might enjoy this trip!"

Rupert soon became quite used to the noise of the jets, and before long the two friends were exchanging shouts of wonder at the distances they could see and the tiny houses

trees, hedges and fields below.

At last, Pong-Ping pointed to a glittering patch of blue ahead, and Rupert leaned forward eagerly, as he watched a town flash past beneath them.

"Oooh, I know that place," he cried. "Isn't it Sandy Bay?"

"That's right," called Pong-Ping. "And now we've got a long trip over the sea to reach Nexdor."

The go-anywhere-car surged ahead, passing through banks of high cloud as it began its crossing over the wide, sparkling sea.

After a while, Pong-Ping shouted to Rupert that he was getting hungry, and searching amongst the luggage, Rupert found the sandwiches and cake that they had carefully packed earlier.

"Are we nearly there yet?" he called to his little friend, as he passed him a sandwich.

"Well, it can't be far now," replied Pong-Ping, between mouthfuls. 'Yes, look over there!" he exclaimed, and pointed to where Rupert could just make out the lines of a great mountain range looming up.

"Do we have to cross those mountains?" asked Rupert in dismay. "They look awfully high, and very jagged to me."

"This machine will manage the mountains very well," replied Pong-Ping. "Just trust me. We'll have to go a bit higher though, so hold tight!"

As the car rose into the cooler air, Rupert shivered. "Brr-rr, it's chilly up here," he murmured, as he noticed ice forming on the sides of the car. "I hope these mountains don't stretch very far."

Just as he began to get very cold indeed the machine suddenly dipped down and Rupert saw that they were safely over the peaks. Pong-Ping started to guide the car down towards a green valley.

"This is it," he called excitedly, turning in his seat. "We're in Nexdor, now! It's only a tiny country, so we'd better land as soon as possible. I think we'll try that village right ahead of us."

The little peke switched the engines to low power and the go-anywhere-car glided gently down towards the village.

Already people were gathering in little groups to watch the strange arrival, and they looked on in amazement while Pong-Ping landed his car right in the middle of the village square.

Rupert glanced nervously at his friend.

"What shall we say to them?" he whispered. "Do you think they will understand? They don't look very friendly to me."

"Let's try," grinned Pong-Ping, who didn't seem at all afraid. Boldly he called out, "Greetings to you all."

Straight away the talking stopped and the crowd just stared at the two pals in silence. Pong-Ping climbed down from the car and Rupert followed him anxiously. "Oh dear," he whispered, "those big hats make them look like bandits. I do hope they're not."

Pong-Ping took no notice and walked straight up to an important-looking man at the front of the crowd.

"We have come to your country to look for dragons," he said, speaking slowly and clearly. "Can you tell me where to find them?"

"It is good that you speak to me," said the big man. "My people do not understand. Si, si, stranger, the dragons you seek are in those mountains." He pointed to the towering range of mountains which the go-anywhere-car had crossed when it reached Nexdor.

"Please tell me more about these dragons," Pong-Ping said. "Do they really breathe flashes and sparks?"

"Ah, you know about that," said the man, with a strange expression on his face. He dropped his voice to a whisper. "We call them the Flash Dragons. None of my people go near them. They say the dragons breathe magic into the ground. Only one has ever been brave enough to be their keeper. He is the tall little man, and you will meet him on your expedition.

That is all I can tell you. Now go and seek the dragons. Good luck. You are very brave."

The two little pals walked slowly back to the car. Rupert felt very uneasy at the man's story. "I think these dragons sound very dangerous," he said slowly. "Pong-Ping, are you sure we should go on? And how can a little man be tall?" he added, with a puzzled frown.

Pong-Ping laughed. "Don't be silly," he said. "Of course the dragons aren't dangerous, Rupert. It's just a village tale. And as for the tall little man, we'll know more when we see him."

Reluctantly Rupert climbed back into the car behind his friend, and revving the engine, they roared off up a steep narrow track, heading towards the heart of the mountains, and scattering rocks and boulders as they went. After following a twisting track for some time, they reached a deep gorge spanned by a footbridge. Pong-Ping brought the car to a standstill and Rupert leapt out to look around.

"Oh dear," he called, "there's no other way across this great gap. What shall we do now?"

Pong-Ping clambered down from his machine and joined Rupert beside the bridge.

"Well," he declared, scratching his head, "this bridge certainly isn't strong enough to take my car, and even if it flew across, there isn't enough flat ground on the other side for a safe landing."

"Then we'll have to leave the car here and walk the rest of the way," said Rupert. He started off across the bridge with his friend following. Pong-Ping was carrying a small box which he'd brought with him out of the car.

"I've got the collar and chain and the special food," he said. "All we need now is a dragon!"

CHAPTER 4

Halfway across the ravine, the two little pals noticed a large board which was standing on the far side of the footbridge.

"Look, there's a picture of a dragon on it," murmured Rupert. "D-do you think it's a warning? A sort of Beware-of-the-Dragons notice?"

"No, no," said Pong-Ping hastily. "There's nothing to be frightened of. It's just to tell the people that this is dragon country, I suppose."

Rupert wasn't at all sure that he was happy with this explanation, and the next moment he clutched Pong-Ping's arm.

'Ooh, there's someone strange coming to meet us," he whispered. "Why do you think he's walking on stilts?"

Pong-Ping looked excited. "He must be the keeper of the dragons, Rupert," he exclaimed. "The village man said there was no one else here. Don't you see? That's why he's called the tall little man. He *is* little, but the stilts make him look tall!"

Pong-Ping was so eager to greet the newcomer that he pushed past Rupert and jumped off the end of the footbridge. But the moment he stepped on to the ground, he started hopping about like a mad thing.

"Ooh! Ow! Ooooh!" he squealed. "It's like pins and needles! I can't keep still! Oooh! Help! Rupert!"

Poor Pong-Ping was in no state to explain, but just kept on dancing around and yelling as sparks and flashes shot from beneath his feet.

Eventually, with a desperate effort, he flung himself on to the footbridge and lay there, gasping, "Oooh, it was awful! Awful!"

Rupert was still mystified by all this strange behaviour, but he waited until his chum had recovered enough to get to his knees, and then, in a worried voice, he asked what had happened. "Why were all those sparks coming from under your feet?" he said.

Pong-Ping shook his head feebly. "I don't know Rupert," he muttered. "I was tingling all over. I'm not going there again . . ." He broke off and blinked at his pal. "That's odd," he remarked, struggling to his feet, "you're standing on the same ground, Rupert, but nothing's wrong with *you*!"

At that moment the two chums heard a quiet voice close beside them.

"Welcome, strangers. It is not often that I have visitors," said the man on stilts. The two friends had completely forgotten about him in their anxiety over Pong-Ping's unexpected trouble.

Pong-Ping pushed Rupert forward. "You

speak to him," he urged. "I'm not moving off this bridge!"

Rupert walked timidly up to the man. "Please," he said, "we've come to find one of the Flash Dragons and——" His words trailed away as the keeper peered closely at him and said, "How can the small bear walk in safety? Does he not feel dragon magic in the ground?"

A cry from Pong-Ping interrupted him, and Rupert swung round.

"Why, that's it, of course," said the little peke excitedly.

"Those dragons breathe electric sparks and flashes. And it all gets stored in the ground. That's why I had an electric shock when I walked about. But *you* didn't feel anything, Rupert, because you're wearing *rubber* boots!"

The dragon-keeper smiled in amazement. "Please hold up one leg, little bear," he said. "I must see these wonderful boots."

"They're only ordinary ones," laughed Rupert.

"I have never seen such an amazing thing," exclaimed the keeper. "You can walk about and yet not feel the dragon magic in the ground. As your friend has none," he said at last, "he must use sticks for safety, as I do. Come, we will soon find him a pair."

Walking awkwardly, he led Rupert to a nearby hut, where some spare stilts were stacked against a wall. Rupert quickly chose two of the right size. "I'll go ahead," he said, "so that my chum can try them."

He shouldered the stilts and ran back to the footbridge.

"Look what the dragon-keeper has given me," he said to Pong-Ping, who still sat looking rather glum. "Now you'll be able to walk about without getting shocks."

Pong-Ping pulled a face. "H'mm, I'm not sure it's as easy as that," he muttered. "I've never used them before."

The little bear helped his pal climb on to the stilts.

"I know I shall fall," gasped Pong-Ping.

"Ooopsa! Quick, take me back!" Just as he was about to totter over, Rupert pulled him on to the bridge.

"Whew! You don't expect me to use those things, do you?" said the peke, as he lay sprawled out on the bridge. "Stilts may be all right for that dragon-keeper, But I'd *never* manage them."

Rupert looked dismayed. "But what else can you do?" he said. "You can't walk on this ground without getting shocks. And if we're going to find one of the dragons . . ."

Pong-Ping didn't let him finish. "I'll stay here," he declared. "You'll just have to go on the dragon hunt without me. Here, you'll need the things." He opened the box containing the collar and chain and the dragon food.

"I don't know anything about catching dragons. I don't want to go without you," faltered Rupert.

But Pong-Ping wouldn't hear of any excuses and refused to change his mind. "I'm not moving from this bridge," he said firmly. "It's up to you, Rupert. You simply coax one of the dragons towards you with that bit of food, and then you put the collar on it."

By this time the dragon-keeper had arrived after making his way slowly back to the two pals.

"So, your friend is not coming?" he asked, seeing Pong-Ping on the bridge.

"He can't use the stilts," sighed Rupert. "I suppose I'll have to go by myself. Oh dear! I wish I hadn't come on this dragon hunt now."

The task ahead filled poor Rupert with alarm, and his legs were so shaky he could hardly walk. Together, he and the dragon-keeper made their way along a narrow track between towering walls of rock, and presently the path opened out to a broad space.

"We are here, little bear," said the keeper. In front of them was a great pit, shaped like a bowl. "Is it—is that where the dragons live?" asked Rupert faintly. "Do I have to go into that big hole?"

The keeper nodded in answer, and Rupert edged towards the pit. He noticed a flight of steps nearby. "I suppose I must *try* to catch a dragon," he quavered. "But I don't like this place at all."

As he descended the steps he noticed that the walls of the pit were peppered with burrows.

"Well, I can't see a single dragon," he murmured to himself. "Perhaps they are all asleep."

Glad of an excuse, Rupert hurried back to the keeper. "The dragons haven't come out," he said. "What shall I do?"

The keeper's reply sent a shiver through the little bear. "You must go to the bottom of the pit and wait."

Rupert trembled with fear as he made his way once again down the steps into the pit.

"If there's a dragon in every burrow there must be hundreds of them. Oh dear, I do wish my legs would stop shaking. It's all very well for the keeper to tell me to wait down here, but he's used to dragons. I'm not!"

Every moment Rupert expected the

creatures to pop out of their burrows, but when he reached the floor of the pit there was only one small dragon in sight.

He threw the dragon food as far as the length of string would allow. He waited tensely in the pit, and suddenly the place was alive with scurrying, wriggling creatures, as the dragons shot from their burrows and made for the morsel of food.

"Ooooo! Here they come!" gasped Rupert. "And I'm supposed to *catch* one of them. I shall never do it!"

With little jerks, he pulled the food towards him, hoping to separate one of the creatures from the rest. But they crowded round his feet, darting and snapping at the food.

"They'll be all over me in a minute!" he exclaimed in alarm as he backed away, nervously. "I can't stay here!" Again the creatures surged forward, and Rupert, whose only wish

was to get away from them, turned and bolted headlong for the steps, the dragon food trailing behind him on the string.

"What a dreadful place!" he panted as he scrambled up the steps. "Nobody told me it was going to be like that!"

At the top of the pit he found the keeper waiting for him.

"Oh," Rupert gasped. "Did you see what happened down there?"

'Yes, I saw everything, little bear," replied the keeper. "You had great courage to go into the pit. Try again, and you will be less afraid of the dragons."

"Oh, but I simply *can't* go down there any more!" The very idea of facing the dragons a second time filled the little bear with dread. "It was horried with those dragons breathing sparks and flashes and rushing round me."

CHAPTER 5

In his anxiety Rupert had forgotten that he still held the string fastened to the dragon food. And neither he nor the keeper saw one of the creatures climbing out of the pit.

A sharp tug on the string took Rupert by surprise, and he was all but pulled off his feet.

"Why, it's one of the dragons!" he cried. As he staggered backwards, Rupert saw that the creature had the piece of food between its teeth. The keeper moved excitedly on his stilts.

"Quickly, put the collar on it," he urged.

"Will it turn round and bite me?" hesitated Rupert.

"No, no, do it now," said the keeper, hastily. "It is safe while the dragon is eating."

And—click!—in an instant, Rupert fastened the collar round the creature's neck.

"I've done it!" he shouted. He picked up the free end of the dragon's chain. "I didn't think it would be as easy as that!"

The keeper beamed at the little bear, and gazed at the dragon as it quietly finished its food.

"You should be proud, Rupert," he said. "You are the first person ever to catch one of these dragons. We must return at once and show your friend."

To Rupert's great surprise, the dragon gave no trouble at all and seemed as tame as any pet. It followed quietly, and Rupert noticed that it wasn't breathing sparks and flashes any more.

Presently they approached the bridge, the little animal trotting along behind Rupert quite happily.

Pong-Ping saw them coming and gave a whoop of joy on seeing the dragon.

"Good for you, Rupert!" he cried. "You've done jolly well!" And the dragon sat up and greeted him just like a dog!

"I wish I knew why he isn't breathing sparks now," said Rupert.

"Ah, that's because of the special collar," chuckled Pong-Ping. "It collects the electricity. What a good thing you came with me, Rupert!"

Pong-Ping patted Rupert on the back, and then he turned to the keeper.

"I must pay you for that dragon," he said, opening his purse.

"It is not money I wish for," replied the keeper. "If only I had those wonderful black boots, like the little bear's, then I could walk in safety without these sticks."

"That's easily done," exclaimed Pong-Ping. "I'll send you a pair of rubber boots as soon as we get back."

The three friends turned back and crossed

the bridge. Once on the other side they were out of dragon country again, and the keeper no longer needed to use his stilts.

While Rupert looked after the dragon, Pong-Ping took his place in the driver's seat of the go-anywhere-car. Then, waving good-bye to the keeper, they started off downhill at a dizzy speed.

Pong-Ping switched on the jets, and the extra power sent the machine soaring high enough to carry the chums over the mountain tops.

The journey back was swift and smooth, and by evening they landed on the fringe of Nutwood.

Rupert stood up and gazed straight ahead. "There's no light in our cottage," he murmured. "Whatever can be the matter?"

The two chums scrambled out and hurried along the garden path.

"Mummy, Daddy, where are you?" called Rupert, as he opened the door and peered into the hall.

Next moment he gasped in relief, for he could dimly see his Daddy there.

"Rupert," he cried. "At last! What has kept you out all this time? I have enough to worry about now that the lights have fused. You should have been home in time for tea. After all, you weren't very far away." He looked solemnly at Rupert.

"I'm sorry for being late, Daddy," said Rupert. "But we *did* go a long way. We travelled miles and miles . . ."

"Just a moment, Rupert," said Pong-Ping excitedly. "Would you mind getting that dragon for me?"

Rupert went off, wondering why his chum was so excited.

"Ah, thank you, Rupert," said Pong-Ping as

the little bear returned with the dragon on its lead. "Now, we'll try my idea!"

Mr Bear was asked to bring a long piece of electric light flex and Pong-Ping fixed it on to the dragon's collar. Then he put a plug on the other end and connected it to the lamp on the table. At once the lamp lit up.

"Don't ask me how it works," smiled Mr Bear. "Pong-Ping's been trying to explain but I'm baffled. Still, it will do nicely until I can get our lights working."

Mrs Bear joined them and they all sat round the table while Rupert related his story of the dragon hunt. He chattered on until Mr Bear cried, 'Whoa! Mummy thought Pong-Ping wanted to fetch a dragon from *next door*!"

"Oh, dear," said Rupert, turning to his friend. "And we went all that way to fetch it from Nexdor! They do sound rather alike, don't they?" Pong-Ping looked flustered, but they were soon all laughing over the mix-up.